INTERNATIONAL

CRIMINAL COURT AND

Exploring the effectiveness of the ICC and Its Impact On The Rule of Law and Human Rights in Kenya.

ABSTRACT

The aim of this text is to determine the effectiveness of the ICC in general in the aftermath of the ICC intervention linked to the collapsed Kenya case in particular. Kenya, an East African country, has a mixed history It is a former colony of Britain which had a violent process to its independence in 1963 but had relative peace and stability, in comparison to its neighbours. After the passing of one of the key founding fathers, Jomo Kenyatta, its first president in 1978, Moi, the then vice president assumed power. In the early 1990s after international and local pressure, Moi opened up political space to a multiparty system. This led to the election of Mwai Kibaki in 2002 who ruled until around 2013. But it was the disputed election of 2007 that led to widespread violence and bloodshed that led to the intervention of the ICC. The case collapsed due to a number of factors as examined below. This brings into question the effectiveness of the ICC in general and the Kenya case in particular, will be the focus of this text.

Shemi ESQUIRE

By Shemi Esquire

INTERNATIONAL CRIMINAL COURT AND KENYA:

Exploring the effectiveness of the ICC and Its Impact On The Rule of Law and Human Rights in Kenya.

By Shemi Esquire

First draft 2016/17, redrafted 2021/22.

For SJ as always.

23.06.2022

Exploring the effectiveness of the ICC in the aftermath of the Kenya Case and its impact on the region.

By Shemi Esquire

Foreword

This text was first written prior to the recent political developments around the world that shaped international institutions. The semblance of the world order negotiated or established since the end of the second world war. An international cooperation that has been almost routinely taken for granted, in the decades after the second world war, appears shaken if not reversed.

Since then, the election of trump saw the almost near destruction of the entire executive and legislative branch in what has become to be characterised as January the 6th. A date that lies in infamy since it refers to the criminal invasion of the house of congress on the 6th of January 2021. In the midst of a raging global pandemic and public lockdowns.

The political, socio-economic and regional the relationship in Europe has also been reshaped by Brexit, which is the departure of the United Kingdom from the EU.[1]

---

[1] Mold, Andrew. "The consequences of Brexit for Africa: The case of the east African community." *Journal of African Trade* 5.1-2 (2018): 1-17; Mold, Andrew. "The consequences of Brexit for Africa: The case of the east African community." *Journal of African Trade* 5.1-2 (2018): 1-17. Langan, Mark. "Brexit and trade ties between Europe and Commonwealth states in sub-Saharan Africa: Opportunities for pro-poor growth or a further entrenchment of North–South inequalities?." *The Round Table* 105.5 (2016): 477-487.

By Shemi Esquire

Furthermore, the Russian annexation of Crimea, then followed later by a later full-blown invasion of Ukraine has put once again, the ICC at the fore.

On the African continent in particular, there was a coup d'état in Zimbabwe against the long standing guerrilla freedom fighter, turned dictator Robert Mugabe, an insurrection in Sudan, civil war in south Sudan and what has been classified as the most violent election characterised with alleged gross human rights violations in Uganda, by the regime of the almost 40 years. Against a restless and awakened youthful population. The alleged crimes and human rights violations have once again been lodged in the ICC from the same region.[2]

The war/s in Congo still rage on between rebels, militias against the Congo government s well as rising tensions between Congo with Rwanda. The East African heads of states, led by outgoing incumbent Uhuru Kenyatta are reported to have sent or authorised sending peace keeping forces to the country.[3]The East African heads of state led by outgoing incumbent Uhuru Kenyatta, are

---

[2] East Africa Turmoil (voaafrica.com); World Report 2020: Rwanda | Human Rights Watch (hrw.org); Defending Democracy in Exile: Understanding and Responding to Transnational Repression (freedomhouse.org); World Report 2020: Uganda | Human Rights Watch (hrw.org); World Report 2020: Eritrea | Human Rights Watch (hrw.org); World Report 2020: Ethiopia | Human Rights Watch (hrw.org); World Report 2020: Kenya | Human Rights Watch (hrw.org)

[3] Prunier, Gérard. *Africa's world war: Congo, the Rwandan genocide, and the making of a continental catastrophe*. Oxford University Press, 2008. Weiss, Herbert F. *War and Peace in the Democratic Republic of the Congo*. Nordic Africa Institute, 2000.

By Shemi Esquire

reported to have sent or authorised sending peace keeping forces to the country.[4]

Ironically, events in Kenya which remains largely the most stable and prosperous country in the region, have turned full circle. With the previous political friends once facing justice at the ICC, are now in different political camps.[5] With the main running candidate and former prime minister, Raila Odinga, facing William Ruto the incumbent vice president. It is widely reported that the incumbent president Uhuru Kenyatta, has backed Raila Odinga as opposed to his vice president and former ICC subject.

As someone once stated, indeed a week is a long time in politics or permanent interests not permanent friends, since the 2007 violence.[6]

The Kenyan courts have exercised a degree of independence and constitutional valour by overturning an election and a bid to amend the constitution, in the most recent past[7]. Features that remain largely elusive in the region, comparatively.

---

[4] Prunier, Gérard. *Africa's world war: Congo, the Rwandan genocide, and the making of a continental catastrophe*. Oxford University Press, 2008. Weiss, Herbert F. *War and Peace in the Democratic Republic of the Congo*. Nordic Africa Institute, 2000.

[5] The 2022 Kenyan General Election: An Analysis of New and Enduring Violence Risk Factors | The Sentinel Project

[6] Cheeseman, Nic. "The Kenyan elections of 2007: an introduction." *Journal of Eastern African Studies* 2.2 (2008): 166-184.

[7] Const2010 (kenyalaw.org)

By Shemi Esquire

Whether this has a nexus to the ICC proceedings is difficult to judge at this point in time. But there appears to an emerging political and judicial maturity[8] that is missing in Kenya's neighbours mired in war after war with incumbents who have spent decades in power, with no sign of willingness to give an inch.

Even war-torn Congo has managed a peaceful transition of sorts. Unlike, Rwanda, Uganda, Sudan, south Sudan and Eritrea. Ethiopia following transition after over two decades has been mired in a war that threatens its federal statehood.

What is clear, is that the ICC, United Nations and global institutions that have shaped the international cooperation amongst nations is facing multiple stress tests.

It is yet to be determined whether this will stand the test of time.

---

[8] Kenyan President, Election Overturned by Court, Attacks Judiciary (voanews.com); The Kenyan Supreme Court Overturns Presidential Election Results: Of Forms 34As, Bs and Cs | OHRH (ox.ac.uk)

Exploring the effectiveness of the ICC in the aftermath of the Kenya Case and its impact on the region.

By Shemi Esquire

Background

The aim of this text is to determine the effectiveness of the ICC in general in the aftermath of the Kenya case in particular.

Kenya, an East African country, has a mixed history. It is a former colony of Britain which had a violent process to its independence in 1963 but had relative peace and stability, in comparison to its neighbours.[9]

After one of the key founding fathers, Jomo Kenyatta's passing, Moi, the then vice president assumed power. In the early 1990s after international and local pressure, Moi opened up political space to a multiparty system. This led to the election of Mwai Kibaki in 2002 who ruled until 2013.[10]

---

[9] Uganda, Ethiopia, Sudan, Somalia and Congo among others

[10] (PDF) Human Rights Abuse in Kenya Under Daniel Arap Moi, 1978 | Munyae Isaac - Academia.edu; Human Rights Watch World Report 2002: Africa: Kenya (hrw.org)

But it was the disputed election of 2007 that led to widespread violence and bloodshed[11] that led to the ICC intervention,[12] by the ICC. The case collapsed due to a number of factors as examined below.[13]

Therefore, the effectiveness of the ICC in general and the Kenya case in particular, will be the focus of this text.[14]

Overview of the International Criminal Court

Based in the Hague the international criminal court was founded under the Rome statute of July 2002. It has a mandate is to investigate and prosecute [15]'the 'most serious crimes of concern to the international community' with jurisdiction over 'genocide, crimes against humanity and war crimes.[16]'

---

[11] https://www.hrw.org/report/2008/03/16/ballots-bullets/organized-political-violence-and-kenyas-crisis-governance

[12] https://www.icc-cpi.int/kenya

[13] https://www.standardmedia.co.ke/article/2001243072/icc-regrets-collapse-of-kenyan-cases-hopes-they-will-be-revived

[14] Uhuru Kenyatta | Coalition for the International Criminal Court (coalitionfortheicc.org); Kenya: Impact of the ICC Proceedings | Crisis Group

[15] https://www.hrw.org/news/1998/12/01/summary-key-provisions-icc-statute

Exploring the effectiveness of the ICC in the aftermath of the Kenya Case and its impact on the region.

By Shemi Esquire

Recent political situation in Kenya

There has since been yet another bitterly disputed election, supreme court intervention, allegations of intimidation of the judiciary and the boycott of the subsequent elections by the opposition.[17]

In February 2018, the opposition leader has sworn[18] himself as 'a peoples' president and several opposition leaders have been arrested. Some incommunicado, according to media reports[19]. It is that background creates a need to examine the impact of the ICC intervention in Kenya.

Key questions

- What is the history of the ICC and its jurisdiction?.?

- What is Brief background of the history of Kenyan politics?.?

- What was t the role of the ICC in the Kenyan cases?.?

- How effective is the ICC in general?.?

- How effective was the ICC in the collapsed Kenyan cases.

- Has it helped or hindered human rights or democracy or rule of law? in Kenya or the wider region. Suggested recommendations?

---

[17] https://www.nytimes.com/2018/02/04/world/africa/kenya-political-repression-kenyatta-odinga.html

[18] https://www.standardmedia.co.ke/article/2001268404/nasa-swearing-in-will-impact-2022

[19] https://www.nation.co.ke/news/Extremists-capitalise-on-Kenya-political-differences-to-recruit/1056-4291692-tu7xea/index.html

Exploring the effectiveness of the ICC in the aftermath of the Kenya Case and its impact on the region.

By Shemi Esquire

Approach

The text is an analysis of the effectiveness of the ICC in general through analysis of a specific ICC case, its impact on human rights and rule of law in Kenya.

It is largely approached from a legal perspective which used literature or documentary review as the main and prime source which therefore requires documentary text.[20]

Documentary text is a type of 'social enquiry that uses documents as its source of data.'[21] It involves a review of the existing literature to ascertain different schools of thought[22] such sources include books, articles, reports, online blogs, websites and social network sites.

This strategy or methodology allows a pragmatic exploration of 'the totality of circumstances in which the text is conducted'[23]. There was consideration of the feasibility, suitability or ethics of the documentary method.

Sources constituted mainly existing literature such as online sources or text. I have access to online material as well physical texts. I have looked at credible institutions like Chatham house, Royal African society, the United Nations and the ICC website.

---

[20] Denscombe, M (2014)The Good Text guide, 5th Edition pg. 14
[21] Denscombe, M The Good Text guide, 5th Edition pg. 14
[22] Denscombe, M, (2014)
[23] Denscombe, M 2014

By Shemi Esquire

There was a study of contemporaneous accounts of local and regional records like newspapers[24], journals, legislation and government publications or official statistics and text papers the subject for factual analysis, review and recommendations[25].

The advantage of using these sources is that they are 'authoritative, objective and factual'[26]. Although it is important to be aware of the 'type of data'[27] contained in the sources.

A critical approach or analysis was observed to avoid any potential reproduction of arguments which has not been a major issue in this case. However, a factual analysis was the starting point when dealing with historical events, there cannot be *alternative facts.* Essentially events should be analysed from a factual basis even though the analysis may be subjective.

Advantages of the approach followed

There were several advantages of using documentary text.

The main advantage was the relatively easy access to data, convenience and with low cost. This made the text journey cost effective. There was access to institutional records or data such as the ICC[28], case law, legislation and journals from online sources.

---

[24] https://www.standardmedia.co.ke/article/2001267861/different-legal-opinions-over-raila-s-swearing
[25] https://www.ijmonitor.org/category/kenya-cases/
[26] Denscombe, M(2014) The Good Text guide, 5th Edition pg. 15
[27] Denscombe, M(2014) The Good Text guide, 5th Edition pg. 15
[28] https://www.icc-cpi.int/cases

The data used has a reference point with verifiable sources. Such as foot notes, authors and publications. It is also possible to be referenced and it is open to 'public scrutiny.[29]'

Disadvantages

However, there are disadvantages that were encountered.

There was a need to be selective about the information available. Sources and methods utilised to produce the original data, needed to be *evaluated* and ascertain the credibility of the source, data and quality of the information or final output.

Given the lack of editorial control of information on the internet, some information on the internet appeared less authoritative, without evidence and mere opinion. In addition, some articles and statistics, made reference to events or issues that were either out of date or superseded by events, case law or legislation.

The other disadvantage is that when documents are a source of data, they could rely on a product based on other purposes as opposed to specific aims of the investigation.[30] This necessitates forensic dissection of information to remove any ideological or inherent self-interest. Which makes the process more complex and time consuming.

---

[29] Denscombe, M(2014) The Good Text guide, 5th Edition pg. 239
[30] Denscombe, M(2014) The Good Text guide, 5th Edition pg. 240

By Shemi Esquire

'Social construction, *where documents owe more to the interpretation of those who produce then than an objective reality*'[31] can be a hindrance to the way the texter interprets the text. This is because a texter may end up using sources or documents that only reflect a specific opinion or world view, lacking objectivity.

To counter, this potential bias, sources were widely utilised and evaluated to ensure, objectivity credibility by referencing and cross checking any ambiguities.

The other potential weakness here was that it would not be helpful to interview subjects. That would also require further ethical approvals and safeguards which may delay the text and increase costs. If using human subjects, text must be valid, honest and transparent.[32]

Overall, the sources and materials were reliable and suitable for the topic. Accuracy of sources was crucial to the credibility of the text. Information was cross referenced information and critically analysed.

To ensure a well-informed text, there was extensive reading and analysis of materials from a variety of sources. It was important to use appropriate citation and credit as a key approach important to maintain a level of authenticity.

However, the use of documentary produced a lot of information which was similar or equally important and therefore time consuming. This required a proportionate division of time for literature review, detailed reading, analysis, determining the relevance of the issues and arguments, writing, revising drafts and further revision of drafts.

---

[31] Denscombe, M(2014) The Good Text guide, 5th Edition pg. 240
[32] Denscombe, M, (2014

Exploring the effectiveness of the ICC in the aftermath of the Kenya Case and its impact on the region.

By Shemi Esquire

Conclusion

This text question in all probability, will be best answered with the benefit of passage of time. Since legal and democratic outcomes are best analysed with the luxury and hindsight that time allows.[33] But the text provides a foundation for analysis, research and legal scholarship, today and in the future.

Furthermore, the potential weaknesses appear to be either too remote or immaterial in the circumstances.

---

[33] The last year and the current crisis in Kenya and the relationship with the ICC could best be analysed at this moment.

Exploring the effectiveness of the ICC in the aftermath of the Kenya Case and its impact on the region.

By Shemi Esquire

Key Objective

The main aim of this text is to critically examine the impact of the previous ICC case against the president, vice president et al, on human rights and rule of law in Kenya.[34]

Background

The Republic of Kenya is situated in the East Africa, with neighbours Uganda, Sudan, Ethiopia, Tanzania and Somalia.

Kenya gained its independence from Britain in 1963 after almost a century of colonisation. Its first president was Jomo Kenyatta who is the father of the current president Uhuru Kenyatta.[35] Jomo Kenyatta, ruled up to 1978 succeeded by Moi who was president until 2002. After international and domestic pressure multiparty elections were held and Mwai Kibaki became president until 2013. His re-election in

---

[34] Kenyatta | International Criminal Court (icc-cpi.int); Ruto and Sang | International Criminal Court (icc-cpi.int); Kenyatta | International Criminal Court (icc-cpi.int); Ruto and Sang | International Criminal Court (icc-cpi.int)

[35] *Some of the main political actors during the pre-colonial era include Tom Mboya, Odinga and the freedom fighters led by Nick(cite) named the Mau Mau by the colonial era governor or government.*

By Shemi Esquire

2007 was characterised by reports of widespread violence, population deportation or displacement, massacres and general instability.

Following international and regional intervention, an agreement was brokered by the former UN Sec General, Kofi Annan.[36]

Raila Odinga became Prime Minister and Kibaki became president. The violence attracted the interest of the ICC and the subsequent indictment of Uhuru and his vice president et al by the ICC[37].

Kibaki was succeeded by the current president Uhuru Kenyatta who has just been sworn in for a second term after a disputed and sometimes violent election process. The elections were held twice in a short period of time.

The Supreme Court annulled the initial results of the elections which saw the opposition candidate Raila Odinga boycott the second elections held in October 2017. Since then, Raila Odinga was apparently sworn in as the 'peoples president,' in January 2018, in front of a packed crowd of thousands of his supporters at Nairobi's Uhuru Park[38]. More of a symbolic act than a de facto or de jure recognition.

Uhuru, Kenyatta's father was stated to be a political rival of Raila Odinga's father(Odinga-senior). Both of them come from the biggest tribes in Kenya. Uhuru is from the most populous Kikuyu tribe mainly from central region while Odinga hails from the

---

[36] https://www.theguardian.com/world/2008/jan/10/kenya.matthewweaver
[37] Ruto and Sang | International Criminal Court (icc-cpi.int)
[38] In full: This is the 'oath' Raila Odinga took at Uhuru Park - The Standard Entertainment (standardmedia.co.ke)

powerful Luo tribe mainly from the western region. It is the ancestral origin of Barack Obama's father and his extended family[39]. The main town is Kisumu.[40]

The economic situation with pervasive poverty and unemployment pushes sections of the population, to identify themselves, with those they feel will improve their plight. Traditionally, this has led to volatile tribal and religious allegiances.[41] Allegiances which are both emotive and fraternal in nature, to the extent that, no matter the outcome of the elections, the incumbent with a following to look after, is reluctant or unwilling to concede.

Equally the opposition feels that their turn to 'eat' is repeatedly foiled. Most importantly, there is a sense of domination by the biggest tribes such as the Kikuyu. The second largest tribe feels after decades of independence, and their contribution to Kenya in all aspects of life, it's too their turn to have a president.

Following events, there are appeared to be a general sentiment, among some sections of the opposition and other ethnic groups, that cessation[42] from Kenya to form a different country is a realistic option.

Beyond the obvious, lens of normal politics from a western perspective, it is that nuanced and complex mix of family, tribal history, power, the wider struggle for

---

[39] Brown, Stephen. "Our Turn to Eat: Politics in Kenya since 1950, edited by D. Branch, N. Cheeseman and L. Gardner Berlin: Lit, 2010. Pp. 303.€ 29· 90 (pbk)." *The Journal of Modern African Studies* 51.4 (2013): 716-718.
[40] *Just like the two fathers .*

[41] The 2022 Kenyan General Election: An Analysis of New and Enduring Violence Risk Factors | The Sentinel Project
[42] https://www.kenya-today.com/opinion/truth-behind-secession-talk-kenya

democracy and human rights, which might assist in understanding the ICC's case and its implication on human rights and democracy in Kenya today.

This will be the focus of this text, in terms of the ICC's effectiveness in general and the Kenyan case in particular.

The ICC mandate[43]

Based in the Hague, the international criminal court was founded under the Rome statute of July 2002. The statue established, oversight structure over the court, management, budget, and appointment of judges and the prosecutor .The ICC has over 120 signatories with over 30 are from Africa.

It has a mandate to investigate and prosecute [44]'the 'most serious crimes of concern to the international community' with jurisdiction over 'genocide, crimes against humanity and war crimes[45].'

---

[43] https://asp.icc-cpi.int/en_menus/asp/states%20parties/pages/the%20states%20parties%20to%20the%20rome%20statute.aspxhttps://asp.icc-cpi.int/en_menus/asp/states%20parties/pages/the%20states%20parties%20to%20the%20rome%20statute.aspx

[44] https://www.hrw.org/news/1998/12/01/summary-key-provisions-icc-statute

Exploring the effectiveness of the ICC in the aftermath of the Kenya Case and its impact on the region.

By Shemi Esquire

The Rome statue which established the ICC to investigate serious crimes such as genocide[46], also set up the four organs of the ICC include the presidency[47], judicial divisions composed of Eighteen judges in three divisions, registry and the 'OTP Conducts preliminary examinations, investigations, and prosecutions'

In addition, there is a 'trust fund for victims' which supports and provides reparations and help to 'victims.' The ICC has just over a hundred and twenty countries who signed up to the Rome statute. Approximately over thirty countries are African countries[48]. It has a detention centre, a 'seat' in the Hague , a liaison office in New York and field offices in a number of countries[49].

Currently it has preliminary cases[50] and 'situations under investigations'[51]. There are around currently 25[52] listed cases including those that have been vacated[53] such as the current president, Uhuru Kenyatta.[54]

The prosecutor needs the approval of the trial chamber of three judges in order to commence a case on its own initiative also known as 'proprio motu'[55]. Part 5 sets out

---

[46]cpi.int/en_menus/asp/states%20parties/pages/the%20states%20parties%20to%20the%20rome%20statute.aspx

[48]https://asp.icccpi.int/en_menus/asp/states%20parties/pages/the%20states%20parties%20to%20the%20rome%20statute.aspx

[49] 'The ICC has offices in several of the countries in which investigations are being conducted, though not currently in Darfur, Georgia or Mali'.

[50] https://www.icc-cpi.int/pages/pe.aspx

[51] https://www.icc-cpi.int/pages/situation.aspx

[52] https://www.icc-cpi.int/Pages/cases.aspx

[53] https://www.icc-cpi.int/kenya/rutosang#icc-timeline

[54] https://www.icc-cpi.int/kenya/kenyatta#icc-timeline

[55]http://legal.un.org/icc/statute/99_corr/cstatute.htm

http://legal.un.org/icc/statute/99_corr/cstatute.htm

the powers of prosecution[56]. Part 6 to 13 set out various powers from trial, review, penalties and financing, as well as international cooperation[57].

The ICC is intended to complement and cooperate, with 'state parties and non-state parties.' This is crucial in determining how effective in the cases it investigates, such as the Kenya case.

General effectiveness

To assess the effectiveness of the ICC, analysis of its organs and functions is a starting point.

A primary function of the ICC or most courts is to pursue justice. In this case by investigating, apprehending and prosecuting those that commit crimes against humanity. To do that effectively, it has to be impartial, effective and fair, but also seen to be the case by both victims and suspects.

Which means it has to free from political, financial and outside influence or interference, in pursuit of its objectives. In the way its personnel operates, its decision-making process and the policies it executes or makes.

_____

http://legal.un.org/icc/statute/99_corr/cstatute.htm

[57] https://www.icc-cpi.int/about/how-the-court-works/Pages/default.aspx#

By Shemi Esquire

But ultimately its effectiveness is judged on the basis of the quality or fairness of the verdicts and quantity of the cases it handles, the duration it takes, the effect they have on impeding impunity or crimes against humanity among its state parties and the wider global community.

Arguably, based on the Kenyan case, the ICC has not been effective, and it has failed to impede impunity and political violence in Africa and the middle east in particular, including Kenya.

The various functions and modus operandi will be examined below to ascertain the ICC's effectiveness[58].

Key facts of the ICC Case

Uhuru Kenyatta

The ICC alleged that, *'Mr Kenyatta was charged with crimes against humanity, including murder, deportation or forcible transfer of population, rape, persecution and other inhumane acts, in the context of the 2007-2008 post-election violence in Kenya'[59]. Charges were withdrawn due to insufficient evidence. Cases also involved*

---

[58] Totten, Christopher, Hina Asghar, and Ayomipo Ojutalayo. "The ICC Kenya case: implications and impact for proprio motu and complementarity." *Wash. U. Global Stud. L. Rev.* 13 (2014): 699.
[595959] https://www.icc-cpi.int/kenya/kenyatta/pages/alleged-crimes.aspx ; Mburu, Daniel M. "The Lost Kenyan Duel: The Role of Politics in the Collapse of the International Criminal Court Cases

charges against Francis Kirimi Muthaura and Mohammed Hussein Ali. Judges declined to confirm charges against Mohammed Hussein Ali on 23 January 2012'.[60]

William Ruto

William Ruto, the vice president and then Minister of Science, education and technology, the allegations were that *'William Ruto provided essential contributions to the implementation of the common plan by way of organising and coordinating the commission of widespread and systematic attacks that meet the threshold of crimes against humanity, in the absence of which the plan would have been frustrated.[61][62]'*

Independently, other observers such as HRW claim to have made their own investigations which support the allegations made by the court. Other NGO's like the 'Human Rights Watch, claim to have documented alleged violence after the election[63].

---

against Ruto and Kenyatta." *International Criminal Law Review* 18.6 (2018): 1015-1047.; Schwarz, Alexander. "The legacy of the Kenyatta case: Trials in absentia at the International Criminal Court and their compatibility with human rights." *African Human Rights Law Journal* 16.1 (2016): 99-116.

[60]

https://www.icc-cpi.int/kenya/kenyatta/pages/alleged-crimes.asp

[61] Kenyatta | International Criminal Court (icc-cpi.int)

[63] Microsoft Word - QA - Kenya and the ICC 01.25.11 (hrw.org); Our findings are documented in our March 2008 report, Ballots to Bullets: Organized Political Violence and Kenya's Crisis of Governance .

Exploring the effectiveness of the ICC in the aftermath of the Kenya Case and its impact on the region.

By Shemi Esquire

ICC effectiveness in general

One of the glaring failure shortcomings is lack of resources to effectively conduct investigations, protect witnesses and prosecute perpetrators. It handles multiple cases from various continents with complex issues.[64] This would require substantial resources.

The ICC has no police force, and it relies on member states to conduct the necessary investigations, gathering evidence and interviewing witnesses. It relies on the cooperation of member states. In this case, the stated failures to investigate or apprehend the suspects, protect evidence and witnesses[65] arguably alleged to have contributed to the collapse of this case.[66]

---

[64] https://papers.ssrn.com/sol3/papers.cfm?abstract_id=275773

[65] https://papers.ssrn.com/sol3/papers.cfm?abstract_id=2757731

[66] *If the ICC is provided similar powers to the UN security council where resolutions can be followed by the proportionate deployment of security personnel to enforce judgements. In the case of Milosevic and Karadzic it was the local authorities that arrested and delivered the suspects to the Hague. Similarly, Charles Taylor was arrested by Nigerian authorities and delivered to the icc. Ditto the former Ivorian president. ;* March 2008 report, Ballots to Bullets: Organized Political Violence and Kenya's Crisis of Governance; https://www.hrw.org/sites/default/files/related_material/QA%20-%20Kenya%20and%20the%20ICC%2001.25.11.pdf

By Shemi Esquire

Where member states are unable or unwilling to cooperate with the ICC, such as in the Kenya case, the ICC becomes either significantly disadvantaged or fatally incapacitated to proceed with the cases, in a manner that would secure justice for the victims and treat the suspects fairly while conducting proceedings expeditiously. This is a matter of both practical necessity and a basic due process requirement. It exposes the ICC to charges of impartiality and injustice. Which ultimately casts doubt on its effectiveness.

Another hindrance to the effective functioning of the ICC is political interference.

In this case, the alleged subjects were elected to the president and vice president in Kenya. This complicated delicate international diplomacy where a serving head of state could be arrested and prosecuted for serious crimes by the ICC.

The African Union protested, cited allegations of bias, targeting of African leadership . Particularly Libya, where they claimed that UNSC, was using the ICC as a tool for regime change.[67]

There are further claims of a disproportionate concentration of prosecutions or investigations, against African countries. Several African[68] countries have been investigated including heads of state.

---

[67] https://issafrica.org/iss-today/the-aus-other-icc-strategy
[68] http://ugspace.ug.edu.gh/handle/123456789/8602'

By Shemi Esquire

There are criticisms in the case of Côte d'Ivoire-, of the ICC using 'political considerations' as opposed to legal consideration by the prosecutor in relation to the refusal for an interim release of the detainee.[69]

It is also evident that there are elements of self-interest and preservation from some of the leaders, such as in Sudan, Kenya, Uganda and Burundi, where there have been bloodshed, violence and political oppression.

There was a refusal to hand over *Saif islam* in Libya despite demands by the ICC. In Uganda, there are criticisms of similar allegations have been committed by the government in the 80s and 90s.[70]

The ICC point to the referral and evidence being provided by African governments at their own volition as well as NGOS. ICC pointed to the Waki commission which provided the names of the suspects to the ICC[71]. It also cites the cases of Congo-Lubanga and Uganda-Joseph Kony, where both countries initiated the process of their own accord.

However, the ICC appears to have succumbed to pressure from incumbents in Africa and other parties in this case.[72] Witnesses or those that helped to build this case potentially lost confidence in the process and the ICC. That creates a vacuum with no

---

[69] https://www.voanews.com/a/ivory-coast-opposition-to-international-court-release-gbagbo/1788225.html; Deguzman, Margaret M. "Is the ICC Targeting Africa Inappropriately? A Moral, Legal, and Sociological Assessment." *Contemporary Issues Facing the International Criminal Court.* Brill Nijhoff, 2020. 333-337. Arnould, Valérie. "A court in crisis? The ICC in Africa, and beyond." *Egmont Paper* (2017). Mude, Torque. "Demystifying the International Criminal Court (ICC) Target Africa Political Rhetoric." *Open Journal of Political Science* 7.01 (2017): 178.
[70] https://www.nytimes.com/2012/03/21/opinion/in-uganda-kony-is-not-the-only-problem.html
[71] http://iccforum.com/africa
[72] *https://papers.ssrn.com/sol3/papers.cfm?abstract_id=275773*

redress to organised and systemic human right abuses within the jurisdiction of the ICC.

Nevertheless, given the background of slavery, colonialism and neo colonialism, which were based on a racist ideology and resource exploitation, of treating the Africans as 'lesser than,' these perceptions of bias have to be taken extremely seriously, if the ICC wants to maintain its credibility, purpose and ultimately meaningful existence[73]. Some countries have already voted to leave the ICC which is a worrying trend.[74]

The effectiveness of the prosecutor

The prosecutor can initiate a case if a state party is either unwilling or unable to do so[75]. In the case of Kenya, it was Ocampo who initiated the case against the suspects as discussed below. The prosecutor needs permission from the pre-trial chamber. This appears satisfactory on the face of it. However, in the Kenya case, there has been strong criticism against Ocampo which whether proven or not undermines the perception of competence and the impartiality of the prosecutor, and therefore, the ICC's general effectiveness.

---

[73] Nwohia, Raymond. *The Dynamic of the ICC and Africa through the Prism of Neo-Colonialism.* Diss. University of East London, 2016.; Nwohia, Raymond. *The Dynamic of the ICC and Africa through the Prism of Neo-Colonialism.* Diss. University of East London, 2016.
[74] https://www.theguardian.com/law/2017/oct/28/burundi-becomes-first-nation-to-leave-international-criminal-court
[75] https://www.icc-cpi.int/iccdocs/PIDS/docs/ICCAtAGlanceEng.pdf

By Shemi Esquire

Ocampo's alleged or reported conduct

As indicated, reports claim that Ocampo was partly to blame for the collapse of the case. The wider point here is whether there is effective and transparent oversight on the office of the prosecutor. Ocampo, the previous prosecutor was heavily criticised[76] with allegations of case fixing. *Bensouda, the current prosecutor* and the Waki commission seemed to contradict Ocampo-commission' evidence was basis for further investigation.[77]

Judge Wyngaert questioned Ocampo's conduct and dropped out of case on grounds that the prosecution did not threshold of his 'obligation at the time.'[78]

The Waki commission, appeared to support this contention by stating that the evidence at that pointed was sufficient to warrant further investigation which is vastly different from imminent prosecution.

Although this appears to be somewhat contradictory because it was the Waki commission that recommended two approaches. Namely a special tribunal and provided names be sent to tribunal in an 'envelope.'[79]

---

[76] https://www.standardmedia.co.ke/article/2000108707/icc-ocampo-beats-retreat-on-claims-of-uhuruto-case-fixing

[77] http://www.scielo.org.co/scielo.php?script=sci_arttext&pid=S0124-40352017000100007

[78] Judge Christine Van den Wyngaert | International Criminal Court (icc-cpi.int); https://www.spiegel.de/international/world/ocampo-affair-the-former-icc-chief-s-dubious-libyan-ties-a-1171195.html

[79] http://www.africafiles.org/article.asp?ID=19264

By Shemi Esquire

The ICC's position appeared to be bolstered by the delay and tactical manoeuvre by the parliament's vote of no confidence and withdrawing from ICC(insert reference)

More so, the ICC concluded that the Kenya government submission under art lacked 'specificity,'[80] that there was no evidence that the allegations were being investigated and had' probative value'(insert source). It added that it is not enough for a member state to aspire or commit to investigate but required evidence of actual investigations being conducted.

There are also further allegations of internal misconduct and resistance to set up oversight during Ocampo's time at the ICC[81]. This does not instil faith in the organisation and the office of the prosecutor, which adversely affects its ability to conduct further investigations as well as confidence in those it has already conducted such as the Kenya case.

The cases against Uhuru Kenyatta and William Ruto were dropped by the ICC, due to non-cooperation[82] from Kenya and witnesses witness intimidation.[83]HRW puts part of the blame on the prosecutor's office for 'lack of witness protection.'

There were reports of witness intimidation which may not be attributed to the ICC[84]such as exposure on social media putting their lives and loved ones in jeopardy.[85]

---

[80]

[81] http https://www.hrw.org/news/2016/04/15/dispatches-lack-justice-victims-kenya-no-cause-celebrations://grojil.org/2017/11/30/how-ocampogate-harms-the-international-criminal-court/
[82] https://grojil.org/2017/11/30/how-ocampogate-harms-the-international-criminal-court/
[83] https://www.hrw.org/news/2016/04/15/dispatches-lack-justice-victims-kenya-no-cause-celebration
[84] *https://papers.ssrn.com/sol3/papers.cfm?abstract_id=275773*
[85] https://grojil.org/2017/11/30/how-ocampogate-harms-the-international-criminal-court/

By Shemi Esquire

Further observations include 'smaller investigative teams' with sufficient professional experience, single minded prosecutions, 'delegation of prosecutions, narrow focus of charges' and a practice that led to 'false statements' by witnesses in the Lubanga case.[86]

In that respect, criticism of the prosecutor as incompetent or acting prematurely appear to be legitimate in light of the new revelation since his departure from the ICC. Such as his involvement and alleged conduct in the Libya matter.[87] What is regrettable is that there is even an appearance of credibility issues around the office or the person of the prosecutor at the time.[88]These appear to be legitimate.

Beyond the office of the prosecutor, per se, there seemed to be inconsistency on how to proceed. Such as suggestions of a three-tier regime, of high ,mid and lower-level approaches to prosecution. The high level would be dealt with by the ICC, the hybrid would merit a tribunal I and the lower one would be triaged to a truth and reconciliation mechanism.[89]

This creates doubt and preparedness of those who witnesses and other interested parties such as NGO's or witnesses further eroding chances for a successful prosecution . It also undermines further referrals and participation of witnesses.

There has since been disclosure of papers linking Ocampo to questionable internal and external practices, as well as suggestions of strong reservation from judges and

---

[86] https://grojil.org/2017/11/30/how-ocampogate-harms-the-international-criminal-court/
[87] http://www.spiegel.de/international/world/ocampo-affair-the-former-icc-chief-s-dubious-libyan-ties-a-1171195.html
[88] https://grojil.org/2017/11/30/how-ocampogate-harms-the-international-criminal-court/
[89] The effectiveness of the international criminal court and the impact of the initiating entities

prosecutors. Such as ineffective witnesses and strained incoherent legal arguments consistent with the evidence or lack thereof, before the court.[90]

The key question, is why no preventive or remedial action was taken, given the gravity of issues at stake. Liberty of the suspects, international stability, pursuit of justice, national cohesion in the countries concerned and the reparation to victims, among other serious consequences. Does that mean the person, or the office of the prosecutor was beyond the reach of effective supervision? This raises a question as to whether there is effective cooperation between court and initiating authority.

All those shortcomings of the ICC as an institution cast doubt on its effectiveness.

There are other issues such as the difficulty of prosecuting incumbents and the lack of cooperation from member states. Despite an outstanding arrest warrant, no single country that Bashir has visited, including member states has affected the warrant. Such as Uganda and South Africa.[91] This however makes its effectiveness as an institution highly questionable.

Compared to the Lubanga case, where there was a state referral, after the arrest of the suspect and subsequent transfer to the ICC.[92]

The ICC also has to balance sovereignty of member states and its cardinal principle of complementarity. Partly because it does not have the resources to conduct effective

---

[90] http://www.spiegel.de/international/world/ocampo-affair-the-former-icc-chief-s-dubious-libyan-ties-a-1171195.html

[91] https://www.news24.com/SouthAfrica/News/sa-to-defend-failure-to-arrest-bashir-at-icc-20170405

[92]

investigations without the assistance of the state party. But also, it has to respect to a degree, the sovereignty of the countries its investigating.

That becomes ineffective when the member state is uncooperative or is the subject of the investigation, as was the case of Kenya.[93]

For the ICC to be effective, there has to be effective investigatory and prosecutorial powers irrespective of the cooperation of the member state's actions of obstruction or non-cooperation. This could be through the UNSC or regional forces such as Ecowas or SADC in the case of Southern Africa[94] and West Africa.[95]

It would appear that at a basic level of having the ability to conduct investigations, protect witnesses and successful fair prosecutions, the ICC was neither effective nor successful. That is a sad indictment on its effectiveness in general and ability to influence the rule of law and human rights in Kenya.

---

[93] https://www.icc-cpi.int/kenya/kenyatta/pages/alleged-crimes.aspx
[94] https://www.sadc.int/news-events/news/un-and-sadc-conduct-follow-engagement-regarding-strenghtning-support-sadc-force-intervention-brigade-drc/
[95] https://theglobalobservatory.org/2017/03/ecowas-gambia-barrow-jammeh-african-union/

By Shemi Esquire

Impact on human rights/Democracy in Kenya

It was thought that this prosecution would serve as a notice that that the days of impunity, violence against the population and human rights abuses to neighbouring countries[96] *'in the context of international or internal armed conflict'[97]*

In almost every East African country such as Kenya, opposition figures[98] and observers point to the absence of a credible election process. Such as an independent police, electoral commission and civil service.

What follows such as in the case of Kenya or Burundi[99] is violence. Therefore, an independent international institution such as the ICC is crucial to protect lives, limb, property and maintain regional or international peace and security.

There was hope that this would stabilise the country and improve or protect the independence of institutions like the justice system, police or the electoral commission. As well as lessen corruption or violence fanned by tribalism.

---

[96] Uganda, Rwanda, Sudan, Somalia and Congo

[97] HRW observes that[97],*it was opened on the prosecutors own volition,*

Before opening the Kenya investigation, the prosecutor had to seek authorization from an ICC pre-trial chamber. The pre-trial chamber—in a 2-1 opinion— gave the prosecutor permission to proceed in March 2010.'

[98] https://www.crisisgroup.org/africa/horn-africa/uganda/256-ugandas-slow-slide-crisis

[99] http://www.aljazeera.com/indepth/inpictures/2015/11/post-election-crisis-escalates-burundi-

By Shemi Esquire

Since then, there have been two elections, in 2013 and 2017. They were both disputed and saw clashes with the police, some resulting in deaths, imprisonment and serious injuries.

A court decision in the 2013 election, followed by international pleas for calm,[100] kept a divided and fragile peace.

The 2017 election or the period leading up to the 2017 election saw violence, fleeing or resignation of election commission officers[101] and brutal death and kidnapping of a senior IT official of the commission.[102]

Despite serious misgivings, the 'international observers' such as former Secretary of state John Kelly[103],appealed for the result should be respected[104]. The Countries supreme court annulled the results[105].

The judiciary claimed that they were being intimidated. Citing statements from the president.[106] Opposition demanded the resignation and reform of the electoral commissions before any re-run of the election which was boycotted by the

---

[100] *https://www.washingtontimes.com/news/2017/aug/7/barack-obama-calls-calm-kenya-election-violence-ex/*

[101] *https://www.theguardian.com/world/2017/oct/18/kenya-election-official-flees-country-and-claims-presidential-vote-will-not-be-free*

[102] *https://www.theguardian.com/world/2017/jul/31/kenyan-election-official-christopher-msando-dead-before-national-vote*

[103] *http://www.bbc.co.uk/news/world-africa-40905379*

[104] *http://www.nybooks.com/daily/2017/08/30/kenya-the-election-and-the-cover-up*

[105] *https://www.reuters.com/article/us-kenya-election/kenya-court-throws-out-opposition-coalition-from-election-challenges-*

[106] *http://www.bbc.co.uk/news/world-africa-., https://www.bloomberg.com/news/articles/2017-08-02/kenya-judiciary-accuses-ruling-party-of-intimidation-before-vote*

By Shemi Esquire

opposition[107]. Which by default led to the incumbent being declared winner and was sworn in for another term as president with Ruto as vice president.

There was further violence last year after the return of the opposition leader Raila Odinga from the US and Europe in 2017[108].

Around the 28 of January this year, Raila Odinga was sworn in as 'president[109]'. While his deputy and senior advisers or officials claim to have their security withdrawn or under surveillance by the state.

Around the 30th of January a prominent member of the opposition's home was broken into in the early morning hours and was taken away by gunmen, after bullets were fired into his home and a standoff with supporters A court order to release him has been ignored[110].

The state has since the 28th of January 2018 switched off all TV stations[111] with a serious attack on freedom of the press.

Amnesty international reported, 'killings, punitive policing and intimidation amid election chaos.'[112]

---

[107] *https://www.nation.co.ke/news/Raila-Odinga-quits-repeat-presidential-election-Kenya-Nasa*

[108] *https://www.nation.co.ke/news/Chaos-and-gunshots-as-Raila-enters-Nairobi-CBD*

[109] *https://www.the-star.co.ke/news/2018/02/03/how-dare-you-fault-raila-over-oath-nasa-tells-au-eu-and-us_c1707932*

[110] *https://www.nation.co.ke/news/politics/Nasa-to-file-contempt-court-suit-Miguna-Kajwang-Aladwa-detention/1064-4291344-xlolun/index.html*

[111] https://www.nation.co.ke/news/TV-Stations-Back-on-air/1056-4292516-2xuyuw/index.html

[112] https://www.amnesty.org/en/latest/news/2017/10/kenya-violence-killings-and-intimidation-amid-election-chaos/

Exploring the effectiveness of the ICC in the aftermath of the Kenya Case and its impact on the region.

By Shemi Esquire

There was initial optimism has since disappeared. Contributory to that is the collapse of the cases against the leadership. The optimism of a social deterrent effect or an improvement in human rights or democratic norms has not been realised[113].

Another view is that the intervention of the ICC intervention in Kenya may have pushed perpetrators underground, lionised Uhuru and Ruto, due to claims of foreign intervention and heightened the risks of losing elections in the country[114].

In this Kenyan case, the ICC has neither helped stabilise Kenyan democracy or human rights. The ICC in this particular case has been quite ineffective, in terms of justice and promoting human rights compared to other issues·

Although the indictments may have deterred full scale violence in the aftermath of the disputed 2013 elections.[115]

Recommendations

To be effective, the ICC would require both a stick and carrot approach to ensure both justice and the significant eradication of impunity.

---

[113] https://papers.ssrn.com/sol3/papers.cfm?abstract_id=2757731

[114] https://www.standardmedia.co.ke/article/2000091816/international-criminal-court-losing-public-support-on-uhuru-kenyatta-william-ruto-trials-survey

[115] http://www.bbc.co.uk/news/world-africa-21812559

By Shemi Esquire

The ICC could also be more successful if its role were to provide a mechanism for 'reconciliation or mediation.' A view shared by some observers such [116].

The ICC's jurisdiction falls into four categories as stated above. Which require a degree of immunity for those in office to effect any prosecutions.

This leads to incumbents and non-state actors protecting themselves through increased violence, alliances[117] or by staying in power for as long as possible to escape prosecutions.[118] Paradoxically, this creates the abuses and impunity that led to its raison d'etre.[119]

It is important to apply a mechanism where immunity can be limited or be stripped. Or where any diplomatic complications regarding incumbents are not a major hindrance to prosecutions.[120]

The ICC is further limited to working with or in addition to national systems not as their replacement. The rationale appears to be due to the practical impossibilities of a multinational force to replace aspects of the national systems.

---

[116] *ashttp://ugspace.ug.edu.gh/handle/123456789/8602.*Similar to the truth and reconciliation commission in SA after apartheid.

[117] *Beyond deterrence: the ICC effect in the DRC by Michael Broach*

[118] To do so they have to keep an iron grip on the population, civil society and ,limit freedoms of speech, association and assembly or commit further human rights violations.

[119] https://papers.ssrn.com/sol3/papers.cfm?abstract_id=2757731

[120] *More powers would have to be availed to the ICC to intervene as appropriate in non-State parties, such as in Darfur.*

By Shemi Esquire

A suggestion would be for disinterested actors, to take control of a specific investigation in a specific nation, with the full might of the legal, financial and enforcement resources of the UN or other member states or regional powers[121].

That would require political will and having the support of domestic support. This may be too late for Kenya but perhaps it is a model that would be applicable to brewing or new conflicts.

Changing political landscape

This text was first written prior to the recent political developments around the world that shaped international institutions. The semblance of the world order negotiated or

---

[121] ECOWAS[121]

established since and it lawful application which has been almost routinely taken for granted, in the decades after the second world war, appears shaken if not reversed.

Since then, the election of trump saw the almost near destruction of the entire executive and legislative branch in what has become to be characterised as January the 6th which refers to the criminal invasion of the house of congress on the 6th of January 2021. In the midst of a raging global pandemic and public lockdowns.

The relationship in Europe has also been reshaped by Brexit, which is the departure of the United Kingdom from the EU.[122]

Furthermore, the Russian annexation of Crimea, then later full-blown invasion of Ukraine has put once again, the ICC at the fore.

On the African continent in particular, there was a coup de tat in Zimbabwe against long guerrilla freedom fighter turned dictator, insurrection in Sudan, civil war in south Sudan and what has been classified as the most violent election and alleged gross human rights violations in Uganda, by the regime of the almost 40 years, against

---

[122] Mold, Andrew. "The consequences of Brexit for Africa: The case of the east African community." *Journal of African Trade* 5.1-2 (2018): 1-17; Mold, Andrew. "The consequences of Brexit for Africa: The case of the east African community." *Journal of African Trade* 5.1-2 (2018): 1-17. Langan, Mark. "Brexit and trade ties between Europe and Commonwealth states in sub-Saharan Africa: Opportunities for pro-poor growth or a further entrenchment of North–South inequalities?." *The Round Table* 105.5 (2016): 477-487.

restless and awakened youthful population. The alleged crimes and human rights violations have once again been lodged in the ICC from the same region[123].

The war/s in Congo rages on between rebels, militias against the Congo government and tensions between Congo with Rwanda. The East African heads of state led by outgoing incumbent Uhuru Kenyatta are reported to have sent or authorised sending peace keeping forces to the country.[124]

Incidentally, events in Kenya which remains largely the most stable and prosperous country in the region, have turned full circle. With the previous political friends once facing justice at the ICC, are now in different political camps[125].

With the main running candidate and former prime minister, Raila Odinga, facing William Ruto the incumbent vice president. It is widely reported that the incumbent president Uhuru Kenyatta, has backed Raila Odinga as opposed to his vice president and former ICC subject. As someone once stated, indeed a week is a long time in politics or permanent interests not permanent friends, since the 2007 violence.[126]

---

[123] East Africa Turmoil (voaafrica.com); World Report 2020: Rwanda | Human Rights Watch (hrw.org); Defending Democracy in Exile: Understanding and Responding to Transnational Repression (freedomhouse.org); World Report 2020: Uganda | Human Rights Watch (hrw.org); World Report 2020: Eritrea | Human Rights Watch (hrw.org); World Report 2020: Ethiopia | Human Rights Watch (hrw.org); World Report 2020: Kenya | Human Rights Watch (hrw.org)

[124] Prunier, Gérard. *Africa's world war: Congo, the Rwandan genocide, and the making of a continental catastrophe*. Oxford University Press, 2008. Weiss, Herbert F. *War and Peace in the Democratic Republic of the Congo*. Nordic Africa Institute, 2000.

[125] The 2022 Kenyan General Election: An Analysis of New and Enduring Violence Risk Factors | The Sentinel Project

[126] Cheeseman, Nic. "The Kenyan elections of 2007: an introduction." *Journal of Eastern African Studies* 2.2 (2008): 166-184.

Exploring the effectiveness of the ICC in the aftermath of the Kenya Case and its impact on the region.

By Shemi Esquire

The Kenyan courts have exercised a degree of independence and constitutional valour by overturning an election and a bid to amend the constitution, in the most recent past[127]. Features that remain largely elusive in the region, comparatively.

Whether this has a nexus to the ICC proceedings is difficult to judge at this point in time. But there appears to an emerging political and judicial maturity[128] that is missing in Kenya's neighbours mired in war after war with incumbents who have spent decades in power, with no sign of willingness to give an inch.

Even war-torn Congo has managed a peaceful transition of sorts. Unlike, Rwanda, Uganda, Sudan, south Sudan and Eritrea. Ethiopia following transition after over two decades has been mired in a war that threatens its federal statehood.

What is clear, is that the ICC, United Nations and global institutions that have shaped the international cooperation amongst nations is facing multiple stress tests.

It is yet to be determined whether these will stand the test of time.

Perhaps more important now than before, is the fierce urgency of a need for the enhancement of legal and political knowledge on the subject at hand, sufficient for future writing or reference on the subject. Highlighting, the interplay of the legal and the political dimensions.

---

[127] Const2010 (kenyalaw.org)
[128] Kenyan President, Election Overturned by Court, Attacks Judiciary (voanews.com); The Kenyan Supreme Court Overturns Presidential Election Results: Of Forms 34As, Bs and Cs | OHRH (ox.ac.uk)

By Shemi Esquire

In the Kenyan case, it will be for others to make a judgement whether the political outweighed and overpowered the legal.

Conclusion

Ultimately, it is the local population that have to protect their democracies, freedoms and political stability. International assistance can be helpful to a limited extent as appropriate but can only achieve little without the political will and support of the citizens. In Zimbabwe[129] it was ultimately a local solution aided by regional powers that ousted Mugabe out of power. Ditto, the Republic of Côte d'Ivoire, Liberia, Tunisia and Sierra Leone.

A suggestion would be a transitional use of regional forces such as Ecowas, SADC, NATO, as appropriate, with the full legal authority of the UNSC. This has its weaknesses such as accusations of political witch hunt and regime change. But in the case, of Gambia, DRC , Lesotho and to an extent Zimbabwe, have proven more effective, than the paper threats of a court based in Hague[130].

Texters report a mixture of results[131] that would appear to fit into the current state of affairs in Kenya. But the current struggle for democracy and human rights in Kenya is led by local efforts[132], the ICC having tried and failed.

---

[129] *https://bulawayo24.com/index-id-news-sc-national-byo-127411.html*

[130] https://www.brookings.edu/on-the-record/the-role-of-regional-organizations-ecowas/

.

[132] *http://theconversation.com/why-odingas-resistance-movement-could-be-important-for-democracy-in-kenya-86562*

By Shemi Esquire

In this case, the ICC appears to have been largely ineffective. The same faultiness still exists in its current form although the appointment of a new prosecutor, since then may have offered potential improvements.[133]

Unless the ICC has the ability to independently investigate, prosecute and enforce decisions, it faces questions of effectiveness and potential survival. The Kenyan case highlighted its failures in pursuing suspects, protecting witnesses, preserving evidence and managing a credible prosecutorial strategy.

The allegations and criticisms of the prosecutor and his office, in the Kenya case, pause an existential threat to the ICC's legitimacy and credibility.

References

1. Denscombe, M. (2014) The Good Text Guide, 5th edition, chapter 15, Maidenhead: Open University Press. Denscombe, M (2014), the good text Guide, 5th edition, in the introduction, pg. 1

---

[133] https://www.icc-cpi.int/Pages/item.aspx?name=pr1177

Exploring the effectiveness of the ICC in the aftermath of the Kenya Case and its impact on the region.

By Shemi Esquire

2. The Rome Statute of the International Criminal Court | American Journal of International Law | Cambridge Core

3. https://www.icc-cpi.int/about/how-the-court-works/Pages/default.aspx#

4. https://www.hrw.org/news/1998/12/01/summary-key-provisions-icc-statute

5. RS-Eng.pdf (icc-cpi.int)

6. [1]http://legal.un.org/icc/statute/99_corr/cstatute.htm

7. https://www.icc-cpi.int/about/how-the-court-works/Pages/default.aspx

8. *https://www.opendemocracy.net/openglobalrights/yvonne-m-dutton-tessa-alleblas/lessons-from-kenya-unpacking-icc-s-deterrent-effect*

9. *https://www.crisisgroup.org/africa/central-africa/central-african-republic/international-criminal-court-success-or-failure*

10. *https://www.icc-cpi.int/*

11. *https://www.chathamhouse.org/publications/papers/view/193415*

12. *Beyond deterrence: the ICC effect in the DRC by Michael Broach*

13. *https://en.wikipedia.org/wiki/International_Criminal_Court_investigation_in_Kenya*

14. *Kenya Balancing Act: Human Rights, Civil society Neo colonialism civil society and democracy.https://www.huffingtonpost.com/daniel-benhorin/kenya-balancing-act-human_b_3268216.html*

15. *http://www.bbc.co.uk/news/world-africa-40905379*

16. [1] *http://www.nybooks.com/daily/2017/08/30/kenya-the-election-and-the-cover-up*

Exploring the effectiveness of the ICC in the aftermath of the Kenya Case and its impact on the region.

By Shemi Esquire

17.[1] *https://www.reuters.com/article/us-kenya-election/kenya-court-throws-out-opposition-coalition-from-election-challenges-*

18.[1] *http://www.bbc.co.uk/news/world-africa-.,*

    https://www.bloomberg.com/news/articles/2017-08-02/kenya-judiciary-accuses-ruling-party-of-intimidation-before-vote

19.[1] *https://www.nation.co.ke/news/Raila-Odinga-quits-repeat-presidential-election-Kenya-Nasa*

20.[1] *https://www.nation.co.ke/news/Chaos-and-gunshots-as-Raila-enters-Nairobi-CBD*

21.[1] *https://www.the-star.co.ke/news/2018/02/03/how-dare-you-fault-raila-over-oath-nasa-tells-au-eu-and-us_c1707932*

22.[1] *https://www.nation.co.ke/news/politics/Nasa-to-file-contempt-court-suit-Miguna-Kajwang-Aladwa-detention/1064-4291344-xlolun/index.html*

23.[1] https://www.nation.co.ke/news/TV-Stations-Back-on-air/1056-4292516-2xuyuw/index.html

24.[1] https://www.amnesty.org/en/latest/news/2017/10/kenya-violence-killings-and-intimidation-amid-election-chaos/

25.[1] https://papers.ssrn.com/sol3/papers.cfm?abstract_id=2757731

26. http://ugspace.ug.edu.gh/handle/123456789/8602'

27. *https://www.crisisgroup.org/africa/horn-africa/uganda/256-ugandas-slow-slide-crisis*

28.[1] *http://www.aljazeera.com/indepth/inpictures/2015/11/post-election-crisis-escalates-burundi-*

Exploring the effectiveness of the ICC in the aftermath of the Kenya Case and its impact on the region.

By Shemi Esquire

29. [1] *https://www.washingtontimes.com/news/2017/aug/7/barack-obama-calls-calm-kenya-election-violence-ex/*

30. [1] *https://www.theguardian.com/world/2017/oct/18/kenya-election-official-flees-country-and-claims-presidential-vote-will-not-be-free*

31. [1] *https://www.theguardian.com/world/2017/jul/31/kenyan-election-official-christopher-msando-dead-before-national-vote*

32. More than political tools: The police and post-election violence in Kenya: African Security Review: Vol 20, No 4 (tandfonline.com)

33. big fish won't fry themselves: Criminal accountability for post-election violence in Kenya | African Affairs | Oxford Academic (oup.com)

34. The legacy of the white highlands: Land rights, ethnicity and the post-2007 election violence in Kenya: Journal of Contemporary African Studies: Vol 27, No 3 (tandfonline.com)

35. The Political Economy of Reforms in Kenya: The Post-2007 Election Violence and a New Constitution | African Studies Review | Cambridge Core

www.ingramcontent.com/pod-product-compliance
Lightning Source LLC
Chambersburg PA
CBHW081057170526
45166CB00006B/2101